For my great-nephew Thomas Mitton – J.M.

I See the Moon copyright © Frances Lincoln Limited 2010
Text copyright © Jacqueline Mitton 2010
Illustrations copyright © Erika Pal 2010

First published in Great Britain in 2010 and in the USA in 2011 by
Frances Lincoln Children's Books, 4 Torriano Mews,
Torriano Avenue, London NW5 2RZ
www.franceslincoln.com

A catalogue record for this book is available from the British Library.

ISBN 978-1-84507-633-7

Illustrated with watercolour and inks

Printed in Dongguan, Guangdong, China by Toppan Leefung in July 2010

1 2 3 4 5 6 7 8 9

I SEE THE MOON

Jacqueline Mitton • Erika Pal

F

FRANCES LINCOLN
CHILDREN'S BOOKS

What is the Moon like tonight?
Will it look as round as a shiny balloon, floating
way up high? Or will there be a crescent
like a silver saucer, low down in the sky?

The Moon can be so different every time you see it.
What is its colour? What is its shape? Can you even see
it by day? Come on – let's take a peep outside. But let's
be quiet. Others might be looking too.

Rabbit scrambles out of his burrow. It's safer for him now
the Sun has set. Over in the west, near where the Sun went down,
Rabbit sees the Moon. It's a crescent shape – thin and curvy
and bright! Rabbit is busy nibbling the grass. He doesn't notice
that the whole of the round Moon is shining ever so faintly.

But in the house nearby someone points through the window. "Look," they say, "it's the old Moon in the new Moon's arms!"

Fox's cubs want their dinner. She stops in her tracks and lifts her head to sniff the air. There's no scent of food, but she sees the Moon in the starry sky. It is nearly round, but not quite. The Man in the Moon looks back at her. His face is plump and his eyes are huge. Perhaps it's a yawn that makes his mouth so round. But Fox doesn't notice him, because the face of the Man in the Moon is only a pattern of blotches.

"Hoo-hoo," says Owl. "Loo-ook – the Moo-oon." How brightly the full Moon shines! It's big and round and fills the night with gentle light. Lit by moonbeams, the ghostly trees cast dark shadows across the ground. On the Moon there's a pattern of long, bright streaks, as if there's been a great big splash. It makes the Moon look like a silver-coloured fruit dangling in the sky.

But Owl has seen a mouse, and gets ready to pounce.

Harvest Mouse clings by her tail to the wheat stalk where she's built her nest.
Her whiskers quiver and her tiny black eyes can see that night is falling.
It's been a warm, late summer day. But what's this? It's getting light again.
Over the field, a great yellow globe edges up into the sky. It's her Moon –
Harvest Moon! It looks enormous sitting just above the hedge. But the Moon
is really no bigger than usual. Eyes can sometimes play tricks!

Beaver is busy. He has a dam to build across the stream, so he's working all night. Beaver sees the Moon, and for a moment he stops biting through a tree. The Moon is full but it's a strange, dark orange colour. Beaver doesn't know it, but there's a total eclipse of the Moon tonight. Earth is casting its shadow through space and on to the Moon. Soon the shadow will be gone and the Moon will shine silver again. *Crash!* Beaver's tree is down.

Brr – it's cold here! There's nothing around but ice and snow.
By a hole in the sea-ice, Polar Bear teaches her cub to hunt seals.
The white, furry coats of the bears glisten in the rays of the full Moon.
Everywhere sparkles like scattered diamonds. The ice has even
decorated the Moon! High up in the sky, tiny crystals of ice tumble
through the air. There's a pretty ring around the Moon where the
crystals catch the light. *Splash!* Polar Bear's caught their dinner.

Spider Monkey swings through the branches at the top of the tall forest trees. He lives up here with his family and he's always asleep at night. So Spider Monkey will never see the Moon – or so you might think.

But the Moon's still up, long after the Sun
has risen. It's often there in the daytime, pale
and white in the bright blue sky. Look carefully,
Spider Monkey, while you search for your breakfast
of fruit. Don't be surprised to see the Moon
on a beautiful cloudless day.

Koala is nearly always asleep, nestled in her gum tree.
But now she's hungry and opens her eyes. She prefers
to eat at night. She grabs a handful of leaves off the tree —
the only thing she likes.

The branches part, and in the gap Koala sees the Moon.
A week ago it was round as a ball. But every night
there's been less of it. Now there's only half a Moon.
The Moon's shape is always changing.
But Koala is only interested in her special leaves.
Crunch – delicious!

The stars have been bright all night while Tiger was hunting. It's a good thing Tiger sees well in the dark because there's been no moonlight at all. Now it's dawn and he strolls out of the tall grass. He walks to the water's edge.

And there's the Moon at last! In the east, where soon the Sun
will come up, the crescent Moon has risen. It is low in the sky
and its glistening horns point upwards. Tiger sees its reflection
in the lake and slips quietly into the water.

The Moon is a world but it's nothing like our world, planet Earth. Imagine being there, like an astronaut.

There's no air or water or life – just grey rock everywhere.
No wind disturbs the dust. Not a sound breaks the silence.
Even in the day when the Sun shines, the sky stays black.
And of course, when you're on the Moon, you can't see
the Moon in the sky! But what is that, all blue and white,
rising just like a moon? Why, it's our Earth – taking the place
of the Moon in the sky!

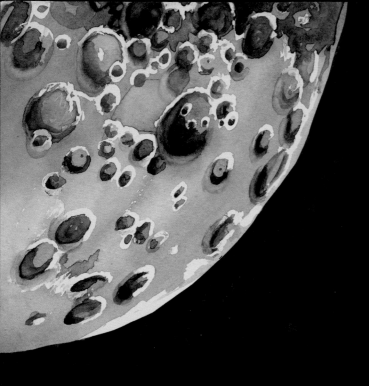

What is the Moon?

Our Moon is another world in space, made of rock. It's about one quarter of the size of our planet Earth. It's about 384,000 kilometres away, which is like going round Earth's equator nearly 10 times.

Through binoculars or a telescope, the Moon looks much closer and you can see a number of round pits, called "craters". Many millions of years ago, boulders smashing down from space dug out these craters. There are thousands of craters on the Moon.

The big, dark patches on the Moon are great rocky plains. They were made long ago when hot liquid rock flowed from inside the Moon. People once thought they were water, and they are still called "seas".

Phases of the Moon

The Moon travels around the Earth. It takes a month to make one circuit, called "an orbit". At different places in its orbit, the Moon looks different shapes, called "phases". We say the Moon is "new" when we can't see it at all or it's just a thin crescent. The full Moon is when it looks completely round. The time between one new Moon and the next one is 29 days 12 hours 43 minutes.

We always see the same side of the Moon. As it goes around Earth, it turns to keep the same face towards us. Astronauts have seen the other side of the Moon and spacecraft have taken photographs of it.

Moonlight

The Moon gives out no light of its own. Only the part of the Moon lit by the Sun shines brightly. One half of the Moon is always lit by the Sun but we only see part of the sunlit half, except at full Moon.

When we see the faint glow called "the old Moon in the new Moon's arms", the Moon is being lit by light reflected off planet Earth, called "Earthshine".

Eclipses of the Moon

A total eclipse of the Moon happens when the Sun, the Earth and the Moon are in a straight line in space. The Moon goes into the Earth's shadow during the eclipse. Earth's shadow is not completely dark because of the atmosphere. That's why the Moon can still be seen during an eclipse.

These are some dates when you might see an eclipse: 21 December 2010, 15 June 2011, 10 December 2011, 15 April 2014, 8 October 2014, 4 April 2015 and 28 September 2015.

Exploring the Moon

Neil Armstrong, an American astronaut, was the first human being to step on to the Moon. Twelve astronauts walked on the Moon between 1969 and 1972 and brought back samples of Moon rocks. No human beings have been back there since but space scientists plan to build bases on the Moon in the future. Robotic spacecraft have sent back huge amounts of information, samples of rock and many, many pictures.